ENCHIRIDION

Translated by
George Long

EPICTETUS

GREAT BOOKS IN PHILOSOPHY

 **Prometheus Books**

59 John Glenn Drive
Amherst, NewYork 14228-2197

Published 1991 by Prometheus Books
59 John Glenn Drive, Amherst, New York 14228-2197
716-691-0133. FAX: 716-691-0137.

Library of Congress Cataloging-in-Publication Data

Epictetus.
   [Manual. English]
   Enchiridion / Epictetus ; translated by George Long.
      p.   cm. — (Great books in philosophy)
   Previously published: Chesterfield Society, 1913.
   ISBN 0-87975-703-5 (pbk. : alk. paper)
   1. Ethics. I. Long, George, 1800-1879. II. Title. III. Series.
B561.M52E5   1991
188—dc20   91-61905
                                     CIP

Printed on acid-free paper in the United States of America.

Titles on Ethics in Prometheus's Great Books in Philosophy Series

Aristotle
The Nicomachean Ethics

Marcus Aurelius
Meditations

Jeremy Bentham
The Principles of Morals and Legislation

John Dewey
The Moral Writings of John Dewey, Revised Edition
(edited by James Gouinlock)

Epictetus
Enchiridion

Immanuel Kant
Fundamental Principles of the Metaphysic of Morals

John Stuart Mill
Utilitarianism

George Edward Moore
Principia Ethica

Friedrich Nietzsche
Beyond Good and Evil

Plato
Protagoras, Philebus, and *Gorgias*

Bertrand Russell
Bertrand Russell on Ethics, Sex, and Marriage
(edited by Al Seckel)

Arthur Schopenhauer
The Wisdom of Life and *Counsels and Maxims*

Benedict de Spinoza
Ethics and *The Improvement of the Understanding*

See the back of this volume for a complete list of titles in Prometheus's Great Books in Philosophy and Great Minds series.

EPICTETUS was born the son of a slave woman about A.D. 55 in the city of Hieropolis in Phrygia. He went to Rome as the slave of the freedman Epaphroditus, who held the distinguished post of secretary to the emperor Nero and later to Domitian. Epaphroditus allowed Epictetus to attend the lectures of the Stoic philosopher Musonius Rufus, who was impressed by the young slave and trained him to be a Stoic philosopher. After being freed by Epaphroditus, Epictetus began to teach philosophy at Rome.

In 89, when the emperor Domitian banished all philosophers from the capital, Epictetus traveled to Nicopolis in Epirus (northwest Greece). There he opened his own school, giving lectures which attracted many students and followers, including the historian Arrian, who collected his master's lectures, probably in eight books, of which four survive. Arrian later compiled a summary of Epictetus' philosophy in the famed *Enchiridion,* or *Handbook.*

The *Enchiridion* is a brief introductory manual on how to transform Stoicism into a way of life. In it are covered rules for proper social and sexual conduct, and for true thinking. Part of right thinking entails knowing how to distinguish that which we can change from that which we cannot. Our lives are subject to many intractables: the vagaries of health and fortune, and, finally, death. But we retain the power to control our thinking, passions, and decisions. In this way we can come to terms with our environment, and thus free ourselves from a world of chance and dependencies.

Epictetus was one of the most important Stoic philosophers of the first century A.D., along with Seneca, Lucius

EPICTETUS

Annaeus Cornutus, and Musonius Rufus. Stoicism's emphasis on reason, austerity, and self-control continued to appeal to sober-minded individuals during the next century (the emperor Marcus Aurelius being Stoicism's most distinguished late exponent), before fading as a school in the third century A.D. Nevertheless, the works of Epictetus as compiled by Arrian have played an influential role in the development of the modern philosophies of rationalism and secularism.

Epictetus died about A.D. 135.

ENCHIRIDION

I

Of things some are in our power, and others are not. In our power are opinion, movement toward a thing, desire, aversion (turning from a thing); and in a word, whatever are our own acts: not in our power are the body, property, reputation, offices (magisterial power), and in a word, whatever are not our own acts. And the things in our power are by nature free, not subject to restraint nor hindrance: but the things not in our power are weak, slavish, subject to restraint, in the power of others. Remember then that if you think the things which are by nature slavish to be free, and the things which are in the power of others to be your own, you will be hindered, you will lament, you will be disturbed, you will blame both gods and men: but if you think that only which is your own to be your own, and if you think that what is another's, as it really is, belongs to another, no man will ever compel you, no man will hinder you, you will never blame any man, you will accuse no man, you will do nothing involuntarily (against your will), no man will harm you, you will have no enemy, for you will not suffer any harm.

If then you desire (aim at) such great things, remember that you must not (attempt to) lay hold of them with a small effort; but you must leave alone some things entirely, and postpone others for the present. But if you wish for these things also (such great things), and power (office) and wealth, perhaps you will not gain even these very things (power and wealth) because you aim also at those former things (such great things): certainly you will fail in those things through which alone happiness and freedom are secured. Straightway, then, practice saying to every harsh appearance,* You are an appearance, and in no manner what you appear to be. Then examine it by the rules which you possess, and by this first and chiefly, whether it relates to the things which are in our power or to the things which are not in our power: and if it relates to anything which is not in our power, be ready to say, that it does not concern you.

II

Remember that desire contains in it the profession (hope) of obtaining that which you desire; and the profession (hope) in aversion (turning from a thing) is that you will not fall into that which you attempt to avoid: and he who fails in his desire is unfortunate; and he who falls into that which he would avoid, is unhappy. If then you attempt

---

*Appearances are named "harsh" or "rough" when they are "contrary to reason and overexciting and in fact make life rough (uneven) by the want of symmetry and by inequality in the movements." Simplicius [*Commentary on the* Enchiridion], v. (i.5).

to avoid only the things contrary to nature which are within your power, you will not be involved in any of the things which you would avoid. But if you attempt to avoid disease or death or poverty, you will be unhappy. Take away, then, aversion from all things which are not in our power, and transfer it to the things contrary to nature which are in our power. But destroy desire completely for the present. For if you desire anything which is not in our power, you must be unfortunate: but of the things in our power, and which it would be good to desire, nothing yet is before you. But employ only the power of moving toward an object and retiring from it; and these powers indeed only slightly and with exceptions and with remission.

III

In everything which pleases the soul, or supplies a want, or is loved, remember to add this to the (description, notion): What is the nature of each thing, beginning from the smallest? If you love an earthen vessel, say it is an earthen vessel which you love; for when it has been broken, you will not be disturbed. If you are kissing your child or wife, say that it is a human being whom you are kissing, for when the wife or child dies, you will not be disturbed.

IV

When you are going to take in hand any act, remind yourself what kind of an act it is. If you are going to bathe, place

before yourself what happens in the bath: some splashing
the water, others pushing against one another, others abusing
one another, and some stealing: and thus with more safety
you will undertake the matter, if you say to yourself, I now
intend to bathe, and to maintain my will in a manner conformable to nature. And so you will do in every act: for
thus if any hindrance to bathing shall happen, let this thought
be ready; it was not this only that I intended, but I intended
also to maintain my will in a way conformable to nature;
but I shall not maintain it so, if I am vexed at what happens.

V

Men are disturbed not by the things which happen, but
by the opinions about the things: for example, death is
nothing terrible, for if it were, it would have seemed so
to Socrates; for the opinion about death, that it is terrible,
is the terrible thing. When, then, we are impeded or disturbed or grieved, let us never blame others, but ourselves,
that is, our opinions. It is the act of an ill-instructed man
to blame others for his own bad condition; it is the act
of one who has begun to be instructed, to lay the blame
on himself; and of one whose instruction is completed,
neither to blame another, nor himself.

VI

Be not elated at any advantage (excellence), which belongs
to another. If a horse when he is elated should say, I am

beautiful, one might endure it. But when you are elated, and say, I have a beautiful horse, you must know that you are elated at having a good horse.* What then is your own? The use of appearances. Consequently, when in the use of appearances you are conformable to nature, then be elated, for then you will be elated at something good which is your own.

VII

As on a voyage when the vessel has reached a port, if you go out to get water, it is an amusement by the way to pick up a shellfish or some bulb, but your thoughts ought to be directed to the ship, and you ought to be constantly watching if the captain should call, and then you must throw away all those things, that you may not be bound and pitched into the ship like sheep: so in life also, if there be given to you instead of a little bulb and a shell a wife and child, there will be nothing to prevent (you from taking them). But if the captain should call, run to the ship, and leave all those things without regard to them. But if you are old, do not even go far from the ship, lest when you are called you make default.

---

*Upton [a commentator on Epictetus] proposes to read "elated at something good which is in the horse." I think that he is right.

VIII

Seek not that the things which happen should happen as you wish; but wish the things which happen to be as they are, and you will have a tranquil flow of life.

IX

Disease is an impediment to the body, but not to the will, unless the will itself chooses. Lameness is an impediment to the leg, but not to the will. And add this reflection on the occasion of everything that happens; for you will find it an impediment to something else, but not to yourself.

X

On the occasion of every accident (event) that befalls you, remember to turn to yourself and inquire what power you have for turning it to use. If you see a fair man or a fair woman, you will find that the power to resist is temperance (continence). If labor (pain) be presented to you, you will find that it is endurance. If it be abusive words, you will find it to be patience. And if you have been thus formed to the (proper) habit, the appearances will not carry you along with them.

XI

Never say about anything, I have lost it, but say I have restored it. Is your child dead? It has been restored. Is your wife dead? She has been restored. Has your estate been taken from you? Has not then this also been restored? But he who has taken it from me is a bad man. But what is it to you, by whose hands the giver demanded it back? So long as he may allow you, take care of it as a thing which belongs to another, as travelers do with their inn.

XII

If you intend to improve, throw away such thoughts as these: if I neglect my affairs, I shall not have the means of living: unless I chastise my slave, he will be bad. For it is better to die of hunger and so to be released from grief and fear than to live in abundance with perturbation; and it is better for your slave to be bad than for you to be unhappy.* Begin then from little things. Is the oil spilled? Is a little wine stolen? Say on the occasion, at such price is sold freedom from perturbation; at such price is sold tranquility, but nothing is got for nothing. And when you call your slave, consider that it is possible that he does not hear; and if he does hear, that he will do nothing which you wish. But matters are not so well with him, but al-

---

*He means, Do not chastise your slave while you are in a passion, lest, while you are trying to correct him, and it is very doubtful whether you will succeed, you fall into a vice which is a man's great and only calamity.

together well with you, that it should be in his power for you to be not disturbed.*

XIII

If you would improve, submit to be considered without sense and foolish with respect to externals. Wish to be considered to know nothing: and if you shall seem to some to be a person of importance, distrust yourself. For you should know that it is not easy both to keep your will in a condition conformable to nature and (to secure) external things: but if a man is careful about the one, it is an absolute necessity that he will neglect the other.

XIV

If you would have your children and your wife and your friends to live forever, you are silly; for you would have the things which are not in your power to be in your power, and the things which belong to others to be yours. So if you would have your slave to be free from faults, you are a fool; for you would have badness not to be badness, but something else.† But if you wish not to fail in your

---

*The passage seems to mean, that your slave has not the power of disturbing you, because you have the power of not being disturbed.

†When Epictetus says "you would have badness not to be badness," he means that "badness" is in the will of him who has the badness, and as you wish to subject it to your will, you are a fool. It is your business, as far as you can, to improve the slave: you may wish this. It is his business to obey your instruction: this is what he ought to wish to do; but for him to will to do this, that lies in himself, not in you.

desires, you are able to do that. Practice, then, this which you are able to do. He is the master of every man who has the power over the things, which another person wishes or does not wish, the power to confer them on him or to take them away. Whoever then wishes to be free, let him neither wish for anything nor avoid anything which depends on others: if he does not observe this rule, he must be a slave.

XV

Remember that in life you ought to behave as at a banquet. Suppose that something is carried round and is opposite to you. Stretch out your hand and take a portion with decency. Suppose that it passes by you. Do not detain it. Suppose that it is not yet come to you. Do not send your desire forward to it, but wait till it is opposite to you. Do so with respect to children, so with respect to a wife, so with respect to magisterial offices, so with respect to wealth, and you will be some time a worthy partner of the banquets of the gods. But if you take none of the things which are set before you, and even despise them, then you will be not only a fellow banqueter with the gods, but also a partner with them in power. For by acting thus Diogenes and Heraclitus and those like them were deservedly divine, and were so called.

EPICTETUS

XVI

When you see a person weeping in sorrow either when a child goes abroad or when he is dead, or when the man has lost his property, take care that the appearance do not hurry you away with it, as if he were suffering in external things.* But straightway make a distinction in your own mind, and be in readiness to say, it is not that which has happened that afflicts this man, for it does not afflict another, but it is the opinion about this thing which afflicts the man. So far as words, then, do not be unwilling to show him sympathy,† and even if it happens so, to lament with him. But take care that you do not lament internally also.

XVII

Remember that thou art an actor in a play of such a kind as the teacher (author) may choose; if short, of a short one; if long, of a long one: if he wishes you to act the part of a poor man, see that you act the part naturally; if the part of a lame man, of a magistrate, of a private

---

*This is obscure. "It is true that the man is wretched, not because of the things external which have happened to him, but through the fact that he allows himself to be affected so much by external things which are placed out of his power." Schweighaueser [a commentator on Epictetus being quoted by Long].

†It has been objected to Epictetus that he expresses no sympathy with those who suffer sorrow. But here he tells you to show sympathy, a thing which comforts most people. But it would be contrary to his teaching, if he told you to suffer mentally with another.

person, (do the same). For this is your duty, to act well the part that is given to you; but to select the part, belongs to another.

XVIII

When a raven has croaked inauspiciously, let not the appearance hurry you away with it; but straightaway make a distinction in your mind and say, None of these things is signified to me, but either to my poor body, or to my small property, or to my reputation, or to my children or to my wife: but to me all significations are auspicious if I choose. For whatever of these things results, it is in my power to derive benefit from it.

XIX

You can be invincible, if you enter into no contest in which it is not in your power to conquer. Take care, then, when you observe a man honored before others or possessed of great power or highly esteemed for any reason, not to suppose him happy, and be not carried away by the appearance. For if the nature of the good is in our power, neither envy nor jealousy will have a place in us. But you yourself will not wish to be a general or senator or consul, but a free man: and there is only one way to this, to despise (care not for) the things which are not in our power.

XX

Remember that it is not he who reviles you or strikes you, who insults you, but it is your opinion about these things as being insulting. When, then, a man irritates you, you must know that it is your own opinion which has irritated you. Therefore especially try not to be carried away by the appearance. For if you once gain time and delay, you will more easily master yourself.

XXI

Let death and exile and every other thing which appears dreadful be daily before your eyes; but most of all death: and you will never think of anything mean nor will you desire anything extravagantly.

XXII

If you desire philosophy, prepare yourself from the beginning to be ridiculed, to expect that many will sneer at you, and say, He has all at once returned to us as a philosopher; and whence does he get this supercilious look for us? Do you not show a supercilious look; but hold on to the things which seem to you best as one appointed by God to this station. And remember that if you abide in the same principles, these men who first ridiculed will afterward admire you: but if you shall have been overpowered by them, you will bring on yourself double ridicule.

XXIII

If it should ever happen to you to be turned to externals in order to please some person, you must know that you have lost your purpose in life. Be satisfied, then, in everything with being a philosopher; and if you wish to seem also to any person to be a philosopher, appear so to yourself, and you will be able to do this.

XXIV

Let not these thoughts afflict you, I shall live unhonored and be nobody nowhere. For if want of honor is an evil, you cannot be in evil through the means (fault) of another any more than you can be involved in anything base. Is it then your business to obtain the rank of a magistrate, or to be received at a banquet? By no means. How then can this be want of honor (dishonor)? And how will you be nobody nowhere, when you ought to be somebody in those things only which are in your power, in which indeed it is permitted to you to be a man of the greatest worth? But your friends will be without assistance! What do you mean by being without assistance? They will not receive money from you, nor will you make them Roman citizens. Who then told you that these are among the things which are in our power, and not in the power of others? And who can give to another what he has not himself? Acquire money then, your friends say, that we also may have something. If I can acquire money and also keep myself modest, and faithful and magnanimous, point out the way, and I will acquire it. But if you ask me to lose the things which are good and my own, in order that you may gain the things which are not good, see how unfair and silly you are. Besides, which would you rather have, money or a faithful and modest friend? For this end, then, rather help me to be such a man, and do not ask me to do this by which I shall lose that character. But my country, you say, as far as it depends on me, will be without my help. I ask again, what help do you mean? It will not have porticoes or baths through you. And what does this mean? For it is not furnished with shoes by means of a smith, nor with arms by means of a shoemaker. But it is enough if every man fully discharges the work that is his own: and if you provided it with another citizen faithful and modest, would you not be useful to it? Yes. Then you also cannot be useless to it. What place, then, you say, shall I hold in the city? Whatever you can, if you maintain at the same time your fidelity and modesty. But if when you wish to be useful to the state, you shall lose these qualities, what profit could you be to it, if you were made shameless and faithless?

XXV

Has any man been preferred before you at a banquet, or in being saluted, or in being invited to a consultation? If these things are good, you ought to rejoice that he has obtained them: but if bad, be not grieved because you have not obtained them; and remember that you cannot, if you do not the same things in order to obtain what is not in our power, be considered worthy of the same (equal) things. For how can a man obtain an equal share with another when he does not visit a man's doors as that other man does, when he does not attend him when he goes abroad, as the other man does; when he does not praise (flatter) him as another does? You will be unjust, then, and insatiable, if you do not part with the price, in return for which those things are sold, and if you wish to obtain them for nothing. Well, what is the price of lettuces? An obolus* perhaps. If, then, a man gives up the obolus, and receives the lettuces, and if you do not give up the obolus and do not obtain the lettuces, do not suppose that you receive less than he who has got the lettuces; for as he has the lettuces, so you have the obolus which you did not give. In the same way, then, in the other matter also you have not been invited to a man's feast, for you did not give to the host the price at which the supper is sold; but he sells it for praise (flattery), he sells it for personal attention. Give then the price, if it is for your interest, for which it is sold. But if you wish both not to give the price and to obtain the things, you are insatiable and silly. Have you nothing then in place of the supper? You have indeed, you have the not flattering of him, whom you did not choose to flatter; you have the not enduring of the man when he enters the room.

XXVI

We may learn the wish (will) of nature from the things in which we do not differ from one another; for instance,

---

*The sixth part of a drachma

when your neighbor's slave has broken his cup, or anything else, we are ready to say forthwith, that it is one of the things which happen. You must know, then, that when your cup also is broken, you ought to think as you did when your neighbor's cup was broken. Transfer this reflection to greater things also. Is another man's child or wife dead? There is no one who would not say, this is an event incident to man. But when a man's own child or wife is dead, forthwith he calls out, Woe to me, how wretched I am. But we ought to remember how we feel when we hear that it has happened to others.

XXVII

As a mark is not set up for the purpose of missing the aim, so neither does the nature of evil exist in the world.*

XXVIII

If any person was intending to put your body in the power of any man whom you fell in with on the way, you would

---

*This passage is explained in the commentary of Simplicius: Nothing in the world (universe) can exist or be done (happen) which in its proper sense, in itself, and in its nature is bad; for everything is and is done by the wisdom and will of God and for the purpose which he intended: but to miss a mark is to fail in an intention; and as a man does not set up a mark, or does not form a purpose for the purpose of missing the mark or the purpose, so it is absurd (inconsistent) to say that God has a purpose or design, and that he purposed or designed anything which in itself and in its nature is bad. The commentary of Simplicius is worth reading. But how many will read it? Perhaps one in a million.

be vexed: but that you put your understanding in the power of any man whom you meet, so that if he should revile you, it is disturbed and troubled, are you not ashamed at this?

XXIX

In every act observe the things which come first, and those which follow it; and so proceed to the act. If you do not, at first you will approach it with alacrity, without having thought of the things which will follow; but afterward, when certain base (ugly) things have shown themselves, you will be ashamed. A man wishes to conquer at the Olympic games. I also wish indeed, for it is a fine thing. But observe both the things which come first, and the things which follow; and then begin the act. You must do everything according to rule, eat according to strict orders; abstain from delicacies; exercise yourself as you are bid at appointed times, in heat, in cold; you must not drink cold water, nor wine as you choose. In a word, you must deliver yourself up to the exercise master as you do to the physician, and then proceed to the contest. And sometimes you will strain the hand, put the ankle out of joint, swallow much dust, sometimes be flogged, and after all this be defeated. When you have considered all this, if you still choose, go to the contest: if you do not, you will behave like children, who at one time play at wrestlers, another time as flute players, again as gladiators, then as trumpeters, then as tragic actors: so you also will be at one time an athlete, at another a gladiator, then a rhetorician, then a philosopher, but with

your whole soul you will be nothing at all; but like an
ape you imitate everything that you see, and one thing
after another pleases you. For you have not undertaken
anything with consideration, nor have you surveyed it well;
but carelessly and with cold desire.

Thus some who have seen a philosopher and having
heard one speak, as Euphrates speaks—and who can speak
as he does?—they wish to be philosophers themselves also.
My man, first of all consider what kind of thing it is: and
then examine your own nature, if you are able to sustain
the character. Do you wish to be a pentathlete or a wrestler?
Look at your arms, your thighs, examine your loins. For
different men are formed by nature for different things.
Do you think that if you do these things, you can eat
in the same manner, drink in the same manner, and in
the same manner loathe certain things? You must pass sleep-
less nights; endure toil; go away from your kinsmen; be
despised by a slave; in everything have the inferior part,
in honor, in office, in the courts of justice, in every little
matter. Consider these things, if you would exchange for
them, freedom from passions, liberty, tranquility. If not,
take care that, like little children, you be not now a philosopher, then a servant of the publicani,[*] then a rhetorician, then a procurator (manager) for Caesar. These
things are not consistent. You must be one man, either
good or bad. You must either cultivate your own ruling
faculty, or external things; you must either exercise your
skill on internal things or on external things; that is, you
must either maintain the position of a philosopher or that
of a common person.

[*Collectors of taxes]

XXX

Duties are universally measured by relations. Is a man a father? The precept is to take care of him, to yield to him in all things, to submit when he is reproachful, when he inflicts blows. But suppose that he is a bad father. Were you then by nature made akin to a good father? No; but to a father. Does a brother wrong you? Maintain then your own position toward him, and do not examine what he is doing, but what you must do that your will shall be conformable to nature. For another will not damage you, unless you choose: but you will be damaged then when you shall think that you are damaged. In this way, then, you will discover your duty from the relation of a neighbor, from that of a citizen, from that of a general, if you are accustomed to contemplate the relations.

XXXI

As to piety toward the gods you must know that this is the chief thing, to have right opinions about them, to think that they exist, and that they administer the All well and justly; and you must fix yourself in this principle (duty), to obey them, and yield to them in everything which happens, and voluntarily to follow it as being accomplished by the wisest intelligence. For if you do so, you will never either blame the gods, nor will you accuse them of neglecting you. And it is not possible for this to be done in any other way than by withdrawing from the things which are not in our power, and by placing the good and the evil

only in those things which are in our power. For if you
think that any of the things which are not in our power
is good or bad, it is absolutely necessary that, when you
do not obtain what you wish, and when you fall into those
things which you do not wish, you will find fault and hate
those who are the cause of them; for every animal is formed
by nature to this, to fly from and to turn from the things
which appear harmful and the things which are the cause
of the harm, but to follow and admire the things which
are useful and the causes of the useful.

It is impossible, then, for a person who thinks that
he is harmed to be delighted with that which he thinks
to be the cause of the harm, as it is also impossible to
be pleased with the harm itself. For this reason also a father
is reviled by his son, when he gives no part to his son
of the things which are considered to be good: and it was
this which made Polynices and Eteocles[*] enemies, the
opinion that royal power was a good. It is for this reason
that the cultivator of the earth reviles the gods, for this
reason the sailor does, and the merchant, and for this reason
those who lose their wives and their children. For where
the useful (your interest) is, there also piety is.† Consequent-

---

[*Eteocles and Polynices, the sons of Oedipus, agreed to take turns ruling
Thebes. When, after a year, Eteocles would not give up the throne, Polynices
attacked the city with an Argive army. The two brothers met in combat and
killed each other.]

†"It is plain enough that the philosopher does not say this, that the reckoning
of our private advantage ought to be the sole origin and foundation of piety
toward God." Schweighaueser, and he proceeds to explain the sentence, which
at first appears rather obscure. Perhaps Arrian intends to say that the feeling
of piety coincides with the opinion of the useful, the profitable; and that the
man who takes care to desire as he ought to do and to avoid as he ought
to do, thus also cares after piety, and so he will secure his interest (the profitable)
and he will not be discontented.

ly, he who takes care to desire as he ought and to avoid as he ought, at the same time also cares after piety. But to make libations and to sacrifice and to offer first fruits according to the custom of our fathers, purely and not meanly nor carelessly nor scantily nor above our ability, is a thing which belongs to all to do.

XXXII

When you have recourse to divination, remember that you do not know how it will turn out, but that you are come to inquire from the diviner. But of what kind it is, you know when you come, if indeed you are a philosopher. For if it is any of the things which are not in our power, it is absolutely necessary that it must be neither good nor bad. Do not then bring to the diviner desire or aversion: if you do, you will approach him with fear. But having determined in your mind that everything which shall turn out (result) is indifferent, and does not concern you, and whatever it may be, for it will be in your power to use it well, and no man will hinder this, come then with confidence to the gods as your advisers. And then, when any advice shall have been given, remember whom you have taken as advisers, and whom you will have neglected, if you do not obey them. And go to divination, as Socrates said that you ought, about those matters in which all the inquiry has reference to the result, and in which means are not given either by reason nor by any other art for knowing the thing which is the subject of the inquiry. Wherefore, when we ought to share a friend's danger or that of our country, you must not consult the diviner whether you ought to share it. For even if the diviner shall tell you that the signs of the victims are unlucky, it is plain that this is a token of death or mutilation of part of the body or of exile. But reason prevails that even with these risks we should share the dangers of our friend and of our country. Therefore attend to the greater diviner, the Pythian god,[*] who ejected from the temple him who did not assist his friend when he was being murdered.

XXXIII

Immediately prescribe some character and some form to yourself, which you shall observe both when you are alone and when you meet with men.

And let silence be the general rule, or let only what is necessary be said, and in few words. And rarely and when the occasion calls we shall say something; but about none of the common subjects, nor about gladiators, nor horse-races, nor about athletes, nor about eating or drinking, which are the usual subjects; and especially not about men, as blaming them or praising them, or comparing them. If then you are able, bring over by your conversation the conversation of your associates to that which is proper; but if you should happen to be confined to the company of strangers, be silent.

Let not your laughter be much, nor on many occasions, nor excessive.

―――――――――――――
[*I.e., Apollo]

Refuse altogether to take an oath, if it is possible: if it is not, refuse as far as you are able.

Avoid banquets which are given by strangers and by ignorant persons. But if ever there is occasion to join in them, let your attention be carefully fixed, that you slip not into the manners of the vulgar (the uninstructed). For you must know, that if your companion be impure, he also who keeps company with him must become impure, thugh he should happen to be pure.

Take (apply) the things which relate to the body as far as the bare use, as food, drink, clothing, house, and slaves: but exclude everything which is for show or luxury.

As to pleasure with women, abstain as far as you can before marriage: but if you do indulge in it, do it in the way which is conformable to custom. Do not, however, be disagreeable to those who indulge in these pleasures, or reprove them; and do not often boast that you do not indulge in them yourself.

If a man has reported to you, that a certain person speaks ill of you, do not make any defense (answer) to what has been told you: but reply, The man did not know the rest of my faults, for he would not have mentioned these only.

It is not necessary to go to the theaters often: but if there is ever a proper occasion for going, do not show yourself as being a partisan of any man except yourself, that is, desire only that to be done which is done, and for him only to gain the prize who gains the prize; for in this way you will meet with no hindrance But abstain entirely from shouts and laughter at any (thing or person), or violent emotions. And when you are come away, do not talk much about what has passed on the stage, except about that which may lead to your own improvement. For it is plain, if you do talk much, that you admired the spectacle (more than you ought).*

Do not go to the hearing of certain persons' recitations nor visit them readily.† But if you do attend, observe gravity and sedateness, and also avoid making yourself disagreeable.

When you are going to meet with any person, and particularly one of those who are considered to be in a superior condition, place before yourself what Socrates or Zeno[‡] would have done in such circumstances, and you will have no difficulty in making a proper use of the occasion.

When you are going to any of those who are in great power, place before yourself that you will not find the man at home, that you will be excluded, that the door will not be opened to you, that the man will not care about you. And if with all this it is your duty to visit him, bear what happens, and never say to yourself that it was not worth the trouble. For this is silly, and marks the character of a man who is offended by externals.

In company take care not to speak much and excessively about your own acts or dangers: for as it is pleasant to you to make mention of your dangers, it is not so pleasant to others to hear what has happened to you. Take care also not to provoke laughter; for this is a slippery way toward vulgar habits, and is also adapted to diminish the

---

*To admire is contrary to the precept of Epictetus.

†Such recitations were common at Rome, when authors read their works and invited persons to attend. These recitations are often mentioned in the letters of the younger Pliny.

[‡Zeno. 335–263 B.C. Founder of the Stoic school.]

respect of your neighbors. It is a dangerous habit also to approach obscene talk. When, then, anything of this kind happens, if there is a good opportunity, rebuke the man who has proceeded to this talk: but if there is not an opportunity, by your silence at least, and blushing and expression of dissatisfaction by your countenance, show plainly that you are displeased at such talk.

XXXIV

If you have received the impression of any pleasure, guard yourself against being carried away by it; but let the thing wait for you, and allow yourself a certain delay on your own part. Then think of both times, of the time when you will enjoy the pleasure, and of the time after the enjoyment of the pleasure when you will repent and will reproach yourself. And set against these things how you will rejoice if you have abstained from the pleasure, and how you will commend yourself. But if it seem to you seasonable to undertake (do) the thing, take care that the charm of it, and the pleasure, and the attraction of it shall not conquer you: but set on the other side the consideration how much better it is to be conscious that you have gained this victory.

XXXV

When you have decided that a thing ought to be done and are doing it, never avoid being seen doing it, though the many shall form an unfavorable opinion about it. For if it is not right to do it, avoid doing the thing; but if it is right, why are you afraid of those who shall find fault wrongly?

XXXVI

As the proposition it is either day or it is night is of great importance for the disjunctive argument, but for the conjunctive is of no value, so in a symposium (entertainment) to select the larger share is of great value for the body, but for the maintenance of the social feeling is worth nothing. When then you are eating with another, remember to look not only to the value for the body of the things set before you, but also to the value of the behavior toward the host which ought to be observed.

XXXVII

If you have assumed a character above your strength, you have both acted in this matter in an unbecoming way, and you have neglected that which you might have fulfilled.

XXXVIII

In walking about as you take care not to step on a nail or to sprain your foot, so take care not to damage your own ruling faculty: and if we observe this rule in every act, we shall undertake the act with more security.

XXXIX

The measure of possession (property) is to every man the body, as the foot is of the shoe. If then you stand on this rule (the demands of the body), you will maintain the measure: but if you pass beyond it, you must then of necessity be hurried as it were down a precipice. As also in the matter of the shoe, if you go beyond the (necessities of the) foot, the shoe is gilded, then of a purple color, then embroidered: for there is no limit to that which has once passed the true measure.

XL

Women forthwith from the age of fourteen* are called by the men mistresses (*dominae*). Therefore, since they see that there is nothing else that they can obtain, but only the power of lying with men, they begin to decorate themselves, and to place all their hopes in this. It is worth our while, then, to take care that they may know that they are valued (by men) for nothing else than appearing (being) decent and modest and discreet.

XLI

It is a mark of a mean capacity to spend much time on the things which concern the body, such as much exercise,

*Fourteen was considered the age of puberty in Roman males, but in females the age of twelve (Justin. *Inst.* I. tit. 22). Compare Gaius, i. 196.

much eating, much drinking, much easing of the body, much copulation. But these things should be done as subordinate things: and let all your care be directed to the mind.

XLII

When any person treats you ill or speaks ill of ·you, remember that he does this or says this because he thinks that it is his duty. It is not possible, then, for him to follow that which seems right to you, but that which seems right to himself. Accordingly, if he is wrong in his opinion, he is the person who is hurt, for he is the person who has been deceived; for if a man shall suppose the true conjunction to be false, it is not the conjunction which is hindered, but the man who has been deceived about it. If you proceed, then, from these opinions, you will be mild in temper to him who reviles you: for say on each occasion, It seemed so to him.

XLIII

Everything has two handles, the one by which it may be borne, the other by which it may not. If your brother acts unjustly, do not lay hold of the act by that handle wherein he acts unjustly, for this is the handle which cannot be borne; but lay hold of the other, that he is your brother, that he was nurtured with you, and you will lay hold of the thing by that handle by which it can be borne.

XLIV

These reasonings do not cohere: I am richer than you, therefore I am better than you; I am more eloquent than you, therefore I am better than you. On the contrary these rather cohere, I am richer than you, therefore my possessions are greater than yours: I am more eloquent than you, therefore my speech is superior to yours. But you are neither possession nor speech.

XLV

Does a man bathe quickly (early)? Do not say that he bathes badly, but that he bathes quickly. Does a man drink much wine? Do not say that he does this badly, but say that he drinks much. For before you shall have determined the opinion, how do you know whether he is acting wrong? Thus it will not happen to you to comprehend some appearances which are capable of being comprehended, but to assent to others.

XLVI

On no occasion call yourself a philosopher, and do not speak much among the uninstructed about theorems (philosophical rules, precepts): but do that which follows from them. For example, at a banquet do not say how a man ought to eat, but eat as you ought to eat. For remember that in this way Socrates also altogether avoided ostentation: persons used to come to him and ask to be recommended by him to philosophers, and he used to take them to philosophers: so easily did he submit to being overlooked. Accordingly, if any conversation should arise among uninstructed persons about any theorem, generally be silent; for there is great danger that you will immediately vomit up what you have not digested. And when a man shall say to you, that you know nothing, and you are not vexed, then be sure that you have begun the work (of philosophy). For even sheep do not vomit up their grass and show to the shepherds how much they have eaten; but when they have internally digested the pasture, they produce externally wool and milk. Do you also show not your theorems to the uninstructed, but show the acts which come from their digestion.

XLVII

When at a small cost you are supplied with everything for the body, do not be proud of this; nor, if you drink water, say on every occasion, I drink water. But consider first how much more frugal the poor are than we, and how much more enduring of labor. And if you ever wish to exercise yourself in labor and endurance, do it for yourself, and not for others: do not embrace statues. But if you are ever very thirsty, take a draught of cold water, and spit it out, and tell no man.

XLVIII

The condition and characteristic of an uninstructed person is this: he never expects from himself profit (advantage) nor harm, but from externals. The condition and characteristic of a philosopher is this: he expects all advantage and all harm from himself. The signs (marks) of one who is making progress are these: he censures no man, he praises no man, he blames no man, he accuses no man, he says nothing about himself as if he were somebody or knew something; when he is impeded at all or hindered, he blames himself: if a man praises him, he ridicules the praiser to himself: if a man censures him, he makes no defense: he goes about like weak persons, being careful not to move any of the things which are placed, before they are firmly fixed: he removes all desire from himself, and he transfers aversion to those things only of the things within our power which are contrary to nature: he employs a moderate movement toward everything: whether he is considered foolish or ignorant, he cares not: and in a word he watches himself as if he were an enemy and lying in ambush.

XLIX

When a man is proud because he can understand and explain the writings of Chrysippus,[*] say to yourself, If Chrysippus had not written obscurely, this man would have nothing to be proud of. But what is it that I wish? To

[*Chrysippus. Ca. 280–207 B.C. A leading Stoic. He succeeded Cleanthes as head of the Stoic School in 232.]

understand Nature and to follow it. I inquire, therefore, who is the interpreter: and when I have heard that it is Chrysippus, I come to him (the interpreter). But I do not understand what is written, and therefore I seek the interpreter. And so far there is yet nothing to be proud of. But when I shall have found the interpreter, the thing that remains is to use the precepts (the lessons). This itself is the only thing to be proud of. But if I shall admire the exposition, what else have I been made unless a grammarian instead of a philosopher? except in one thing, that I am explaining Chrysippus instead of Homer. When, then, any man says to me, Read Chrysippus to me, I rather blush, when I cannot show my acts like to and consistent with his words.

L

Whatever things (rules) are proposed* to you [for the conduct of life] abide by them, as if they were laws, as if you would be guilty of impiety if you transgressed any of them. And whatever any man shall say about you, do not attend to it: for this is no affair of yours. How long will you then still defer thinking yourself worthy of the best things, and in no matter transgressing the distinctive reason? Have you accepted the theorems (rules), which it was your duty to agree to, and have you agreed to them?

---

*This may mean, "what is proposed to you by philosophers," and especially in this little book. Schweighaeuser thinks that it may mean "what you have proposed to yourself"; but he is inclined to understand it simply, "what is proposed above, or taught above."

What teacher, then, do you still expect that you defer to him the correction of yourself? You are no longer a youth, but already a full-grown man. If then you are negligent and slothful, and are continually making procrastination after procrastination, and proposal (intention) after proposal, and fixing day after day, after which you will attend to yourself, you will not know that you are not making improvement, but you will continue ignorant (uninstructed) both while you live and till you die. Immediately, then, think it right to live as a full-grown man, and one who is making proficiency, and let everything which appears to you to be the best be to you a law which must not be transgressed. And if anything laborious, or pleasant or glorious or inglorious be presented to you, remember that now is the contest, now are the Olympic games, and they cannot be deferred; and that it depends on one defeat and one giving way that progress is either lost or maintained. Socrates in this way becomes perfect, in all things improving himself, attending to nothing except to reason. But you, though you are not yet a Socrates, ought to live as one who wishes to be a Socrates.

LI

The first and most necessary place (part) in philosophy is the use of theorems (precepts), for instance, that we must not lie: the second part is that of demonstrations, for instance, How is it proved that we ought not to lie: the third is that which is confirmatory of these two and explanatory, for example, How is this a demonstration?

For what is demonstration, what is consequence, what is contradiction, what is truth, what is falsehood? The third part (topic) is necessary on account of the second, and the second on account of the first; but the most necessary and that on which we ought to rest is the first. But we do the contrary. For we spend our time on the third topic, and all our earnestness is about it: but we entirely neglect the first. Therefore we lie; but the demonstration that we ought not to lie we have ready to hand.

LII

In every thing (circumstance) we should hold these maxims ready to hand:

> Lead me, O Zeus, and thou O Destiny,
> The way that I am bid by you to go:
> To follow I am ready. If I choose not,
> I make myself a wretch, and still must follow.*

> But whoso nobly yields unto necessity,
> We hold him wise, and skill'd in things divine.†

---

*The first two verses are by the Stoic Cleanthes, the pupil of Zeno, and the teacher of Chrysippus. He was a native of Assus in Mysia; and Simplicius, who wrote his commentary on the *Enchiridion* in the sixth century A.D., saw even at this late period in Assus a beautiful statue of Cleanthes erected by a decree of the Roman senate in honor of this excellent man.

†The two second verses are from a play of Euripides, a writer who has supplied more verses for quotation than any ancient tragedian.

And the third also: O Crito, if so it pleases the gods, so let it be; Anytus and Melitus are able indeed to kill me, but they cannot harm me.*

---

*The third quotation is from the *Crito* of Plato. Socrates is the speaker. The last part is from the *Apology* of Plato, and Socrates is also the speaker. The words "and the third also," Schweighaeuser says, have been introduced from the commentary of Simplicius. Simplicius concludes his commentary thus: Epictetus connects the end with the beginning, which reminds us of what was said in the beginning, that the man who places the good and the evil among the things which are in our power, and not in externals, will neither be compelled by any man nor ever injured.

GREAT BOOKS IN PHILOSOPHY PAPERBACK SERIES

ESTHETICS

- ❏ Aristotle—*The Poetics*
- ❏ Aristotle—*Treatise on Rhetoric*

ETHICS

- ❏ Aristotle—*The Nicomachean Ethics*
- ❏ Marcus Aurelius—*Meditations*
- ❏ Jeremy Bentham—*The Principles of Morals and Legislation*
- ❏ John Dewey—*The Moral Writings of John Dewey, Revised Edition* (edited by James Gouinlock)
- ❏ Epictetus—*Enchiridion*
- ❏ Immanuel Kant—*Fundamental Principles of the Metaphysic of Morals*
- ❏ John Stuart Mill—*Utilitarianism*
- ❏ George Edward Moore—*Principia Ethica*
- ❏ Friedrich Nietzsche—*Beyond Good and Evil*
- ❏ Plato—*Protagoras, Philebus,* and *Gorgias*
- ❏ Bertrand Russell—*Bertrand Russell On Ethics, Sex, and Marriage* (edited by Al Seckel)
- ❏ Arthur Schopenhauer—*The Wisdom of Life* and *Counsels and Maxims*
- ❏ Benedict de Spinoza—*Ethics* and *The Improvement of the Understanding*

METAPHYSICS/EPISTEMOLOGY

- ❏ Aristotle—*De Anima*
- ❏ Aristotle—*The Metaphysics*
- ❏ Francis Bacon—*Essays*
- ❏ George Berkeley—*Three Dialogues Between Hylas and Philonous*
- ❏ W. K. Clifford—*The Ethics of Belief and Other Essays* (introduction by Timothy J. Madigan)
- ❏ René Descartes—*Discourse on Method* and *The Meditations*
- ❏ John Dewey—*How We Think*
- ❏ John Dewey—*The Influence of Darwin on Philosophy and Other Essays*
- ❏ Epicurus—*The Essential Epicurus: Letters, Principal Doctrines, Vatican Sayings, and Fragments* (translated, and with an introduction, by Eugene O'Connor)
- ❏ Sidney Hook—*The Quest for Being*
- ❏ David Hume—*An Enquiry Concerning Human Understanding*
- ❏ David Hume—*Treatise of Human Nature*
- ❏ William James—*The Meaning of Truth*
- ❏ William James—*Pragmatism*
- ❏ Immanuel Kant—*Critique of Practical Reason*
- ❏ Immanuel Kant—*Critique of Pure Reason*
- ❏ Gottfried Wilhelm Leibniz—*Discourse on Metaphysics* and the *Monadology*
- ❏ John Locke—*An Essay Concerning Human Understanding*
- ❏ Charles S. Peirce—*The Essential Writings* (edited by Edward C. Moore, preface by Richard Robin)
- ❏ Plato—*The Euthyphro, Apology, Crito,* and *Phaedo*
- ❏ Plato—*Lysis, Phaedrus,* and *Symposium*
- ❏ Bertrand Russell—*The Problems of Philosophy*
- ❏ George Santayana—*The Life of Reason*
- ❏ Sextus Empiricus—*Outlines of Pyrrhonism*

PHILOSOPHY OF RELIGION

- ❏ Marcus Tullius Cicero—*The Nature of the Gods* and *On Divination*
- ❏ Ludwig Feuerbach—*The Essence of Christianity*
- ❏ David Hume—*Dialogues Concerning Natural Religion*
- ❏ John Locke—*A Letter Concerning Toleration*
- ❏ Lucretius—*On the Nature of Things*
- ❏ John Stuart Mill—*Three Essays on Religion*
- ❏ Thomas Paine—*The Age of Reason*
- ❏ Bertrand Russell—*Bertrand Russell On God and Religion* (edited by Al Seckel)

SOCIAL AND POLITICAL PHILOSOPHY

- ❏ Aristotle—*The Politics*
- ❏ Mikhail Bakunin—*The Basic Bakunin: Writings, 1869–1871* (translated and edited by Robert M. Cutler)
- ❏ Edmund Burke—*Reflections on the Revolution in France*
- ❏ John Dewey—*Freedom and Culture*
- ❏ John Dewey—*Individualism Old and New*
- ❏ John Dewey—*Liberalism and Social Action*
- ❏ G. W. F. Hegel—*The Philosophy of History*
- ❏ G. W. F. Hegel—*Philosophy of Right*
- ❏ Thomas Hobbes—*The Leviathan*
- ❏ Sidney Hook—*Paradoxes of Freedom*
- ❏ Sidney Hook—*Reason, Social Myths, and Democracy*
- ❏ John Locke—*Second Treatise on Civil Government*
- ❏ Niccolo Machiavelli—*The Prince*
- ❏ Karl Marx (with Friedrich Engels)—*The German Ideology,* including *Theses on Feuerbach* and *Introduction to the Critique of Political Economy*
- ❏ Karl Marx—*The Poverty of Philosophy*
- ❏ Karl Marx/Friedrich Engels—*The Economic and Philosophic Manuscripts of 1844* and *The Communist Manifesto*
- ❏ John Stuart Mill—*Considerations on Representative Government*
- ❏ John Stuart Mill—*On Liberty*
- ❏ John Stuart Mill—*On Socialism*
- ❏ John Stuart Mill—*The Subjection of Women*
- ❏ Friedrich Nietzsche—*Thus Spake Zarathustra*
- ❏ Thomas Paine—*Common Sense*
- ❏ Thomas Paine—*Rights of Man*
- ❏ Plato—*The Republic*
- ❏ Jean-Jacques Rousseau—*The Social Contract*
- ❏ Mary Wollstonecraft—*A Vindication of the Rights of Men*
- ❏ Mary Wollstonecraft—*A Vindication of the Rights of Women*

GREAT MINDS PAPERBACK SERIES

CRITICAL ESSAYS

- ❏ Desiderius Erasmus—*The Praise of Folly*
- ❏ Jonathan Swift—*A Modest Proposal and Other Satires* (with an introduction by George R. Levine)
- ❏ H. G. Wells—*The Conquest of Time* (with an introduction by Martin Gardner)

ECONOMICS

- ❏ Charlotte Perkins Gilman—*Women and Economics: A Study of the Economic Relation between Women and Men*
- ❏ John Maynard Keynes—*The General Theory of Employment, Interest, and Money*
- ❏ John Maynard Keynes—*A Tract on Monetary Reform*
- ❏ Thomas R. Malthus—*An Essay on the Principle of Population*
- ❏ Alfred Marshall—*Principles of Economics*
- ❏ Karl Marx—*Theories of Surplus Value*
- ❏ David Ricardo—*Principles of Political Economy and Taxation*
- ❏ Adam Smith—*Wealth of Nations*
- ❏ Thorstein Veblen—*Theory of the Leisure Class*

HISTORY

- ❏ Edward Gibbon—*On Christianity*
- ❏ Alexander Hamilton, John Jay, and James Madison—*The Federalist*
- ❏ Herodotus—*The History*
- ❏ Thucydides—*History of the Peloponnesian War*
- ❏ Andrew D. White—*A History of the Warfare of Science with Theology in Christendom*

PSYCHOLOGY

- ❏ Sigmund Freud—*Totem and Taboo*

RELIGION

- ❏ Thomas Henry Huxley—*Agnosticism and Christianity and Other Essays*
- ❏ Ernest Renan—*The Life of Jesus*
- ❏ Elizabeth Cady Stanton—*The Woman's Bible*
- ❏ Voltaire—*A Treatise on Toleration and Other Essays*

SCIENCE

- ❏ Nicolaus Copernicus—*On the Revolutions of Heavenly Spheres*
- ❏ Charles Darwin—*The Descent of Man*
- ❏ Charles Darwin—*The Origin of Species*
- ❏ Charles Darwin—*The Voyage of the Beagle*
- ❏ Albert Einstein—*Relativity*
- ❏ Michael Faraday—*The Forces of Matter*
- ❏ Galileo Galilei—*Dialogues Concerning Two New Sciences*
- ❏ Ernst Haeckel—*The Riddle of the Universe*
- ❏ William Harvey—*On the Motion of the Heart and Blood in Animals*
- ❏ Werner Heisenberg—*Physics and Philosophy: The Revolution in Modern Science* (introduction by F. S. C. Northrop)
- ❏ Julian Huxley—*Evolutionary Humanism*
- ❏ Edward Jenner—*Vaccination against Smallpox*
- ❏ Johannes Kepler—*Epitome of Copernican Astronomy and Harmonies of the World*
- ❏ Isaac Newton—*The Principia*
- ❏ Louis Pasteur and Joseph Lister—*Germ Theory and Its Application to Medicine and On the Antiseptic Principle of the Practice of Surgery*
- ❏ Alfred Russel Wallace—*Island Life*

SOCIOLOGY

- ❏ Emile Durkheim—*Ethics and the Sociology of Morals* (translated with an introduction by Robert T. Hall)